Back to Happy

A Journey of Hope, Healing and Waking Up

By

Connie T. Bowman

Happy Healthy You!

ISBN: 1502768542
ISBN 13: 9781502768544
Library of Congress Control Number: 2014918217
CreateSpace Independent Publishing Platform
North Charleston, South Carolina

Table of Contents

Foreword

We lost our six-year-old daughter in a tragic accident on January 20, 2012. Ellie was a vibrant and beautiful daddy's girl. We've found the way through our valley of grief through our faith and the support of other bereaved parents. Connie Bowman reached out to my family with valuable advice and support in our time of need. We also found that serving other families suffering similar losses has been immensely healing.

Connie is an inspiring leader and example to so many people. As you will learn in her book, she has overcome one of life's most difficult challenges. She's found a way "Back to Happy" and candidly shares her story. Connie's book is a much needed survival guide when life gets tough.

If you or someone you know is suffering through a significant loss, I'm confident that this book has many ideas that will help you find your way.

Todd Nigro
Founder of Ellie's Way, Inc.
Peachtree City, GA

Preface

"Let It Go"

Let go of the ways you thought life would unfold: the holding of plans or dreams or expectations—let it all go.

Save your strength to swim with the tide. The choice to fight what is here before you now will only result in struggle, fear, and desperate attempts to flee from the very energy you long for. Let go.

Let it all go and flow with the grace that washes
through your days, whether you received it gently
or with all your quills raised to defend against invaders.
Take this on faith; the mind may never find the
explanations that it seeks, but you will move forward,
nonetheless. Let go, and the wave's crest will carry
you to unknown shores, beyond your wildest dreams
or destinations. Let it all go, and find the place of
rest and peace, and certain transformation.

Donna Faulds
Go In and In, Poems from the Heart of Yoga

Introduction

Happiness is an inside job. It doesn't come from anything we can buy, steal, eat, drink, smoke, or shoot into our veins. It is delicate and precious and ours to delight in or toss out with the garbage if we so choose. Happiness is our birthright. Babies *get* it. But then sometime early on, we lose that innate sense of abiding joy as we are socialized and trained to be responsible members of the *tribe*. As we live our lives, we get glimpses of it, and we're able to call it up on occasion. When we become adults, that sense of well-being that is happiness can be swept under the rug as we get on about the business ("busyness") of life. Sometimes it takes a crisis or a deep depression to make us acutely aware of our need for happiness. Sometimes a crisis like this is just what we need to shake us awake.

Back to Happy is a book about my personal experience with losing my first child, Meghan. It's about life's ups and downs and how we can navigate them with more grace and ease. It's about getting back to peace after trauma and maintaining equilibrium through the chaos that can be modern life. *Back to Happy* is not intended to help with chronic mental illness like depression or post-traumatic stress disorder—two serious challenges that require professional care. If you find yourself suffering from either of these two conditions, please seek help.

"They" say that losing a child is the worst possible thing any human can endure. Perhaps this is true, but life can be hard, and different people experience pain in different ways. When my daughter Meghan died, my world was shaken in ways I never could have imagined. It was a chore to survive in those long first few days, but I did go on. With faith and time and grace and the love and support of others, I was able to heal and so can you. I promise. We all go through challenges in our lives that test our strength and ability to move forward. We all have different coping skills and culturally defined ways of navigating difficult times. But we are all human and by definition have similar needs: the need to be comforted and loved, to be heard, to explore and uncover the mysteries of life and death.

In this book, I share some of my experiences related to the loss of my beautiful daughter as well as stories of others who have faced struggles and come out on the other side. I give practical advice for healing. I learned the nine lessons in this book by going through my dark night of the soul. I impart them to you in the hope that you will not have to. I also provide links to podcast interviews I have done with many courageous people. The podcasts are designed to bolster your courage and give you hope and inspiration. In the back of the book, I have included some of my favorite books, prayers, videos, and poems that have inspired me through my own journey. I encourage you to take what helps and use it. If it doesn't feel right to you, then just give it a pass.

Here's my first tip toward your healing journey: The final phase of healing is the ability and the opportunity to help another. If something here helps you, please pass it on; you will be helped in the process!

It is my prayer that within these pages you find something that resonates with you, something that gives you inspiration, hope, and peace. These are the things I have learned from my journey and that others have shared with me about their own. These ways that I have found take me again and again back to happy.

one

Baby Love

"In a day fraught with worry over breaths taken through blue lips and oxygen machines, blessings come from the tiniest things. An extra bite of macaroni and cheese makes me want to sing the 'Hallelujah Chorus.' Her smile is my very joy, her happiness my only mission. I begin to live from blessing to blessing. They become bridges over troubled water as I learn, ever too slowly, how to piece together this new way of life, which revolves around a daughter with a life-threatening condition."
(Journal entry: June, 1987)

From the moment she was conceived, I was acutely aware of the blessing that was my daughter, my first-born—Meghan Rebecca Bowman. I am not exaggerating about this. My husband was in the military when Meghan was conceived, and that meant frequent separations. The occasion of Meghan's conception was obvious, as I had paid a visit to my husband, who was away on a training mission. I recall being aware of something different the day after our visit. I felt light, as though I had a secret. It seemed like years passed before the several weeks I had to wait to have the test that would confirm what I already knew. I was pregnant! I was a happy, pregnant woman. I loved the entire experience and lived in a blissful, beautiful kind of place for the whole of it.

Meghan was born a couple of weeks early but was a good size: seven pounds, seven-and-a-half ounces. She had perfect APGAR scores—the evaluation they do right after birth that describes the infant's condition. Not long after that, however, she started having breathing issues, and her color started turning dusky, so off she went to the hospital nursery to be watched more closely. In my new new-mother bliss, I wasn't worried at all. Visitors came and went and brought gifts and flowers. All was perfect, or so I thought. Two days later, the doctors were still concerned about Meghan. We were kept in the hospital and batteries of tests were performed on her heart and lungs. By this time, my mom had arrived to help out for the first few days after we went home. She seemed calm, which helped me stay that way, as well. After four days in the hospital, Meghan and I were going home!

Once we were settled back at home, my husband and I began our new lives as parents to Meghan. Life was sweet and uneventful as we got to know our new little one. I remember feeling as though my heart would just burst with love when I held her. When she slept too long, I would creep into her room to take a peek, wishing for her to wake up so I could hold her again.

Meghan grew normally for the first year of her life. She had no physical symptoms, save for a cold here and there, an ear infection, and some teething pain. She had such a cute personality, and her smile melted my heart. People used to say that her smile was so big, it looked like her face would crack. It was true.

When Meghan was about a year and a half, I started noticing that she was getting more colds that turned into pneumonias. When I took her to the doctor, they would tell me that all kids get sick, so not to worry. This is normal, they said. "Go home, chill out."

I knew that breast-feeding offers infants a certain amount of immunity from colds and flu. I had stopped nursing at a year, and I reasoned that this could account for her more frequent illnesses. As time went on, I grew more and more concerned about Meghan's illnesses, despite the doctors' insistence that everything was fine. She was growing, albeit at a slower rate than previously, and she had no real symptoms to be concerned about, so they continued to tell me that nothing was wrong. About that time, I began to have symptoms of my own.

My heart would beat right out of my chest, and I thought I was having a heart attack. These full-blown anxiety attacks became worse until one day I went in to see my doctor. He knew I had been concerned about Meghan, and he suggested that I take a vacation. He said the stress of being a new mother must have been getting to me. I guess it was.

By the time Meghan was close to two years old, I found Dr. Staub at the recommendation of a friend. He wasn't the most consoling pediatrician I had met, but he knew his stuff. He was all business as he listened to Meghan's heart and lungs, palpated the veins in her little neck, and gave her a thorough examination. I could feel my body relax in his presence, until I heard the sentence that I never wanted to hear: "I think this child has a heart condition."

Conflicting emotions of fear and relief swept through me as we were whisked off to have an echocardiogram in a neighboring hospital. Ironically, as I was taking her in for the procedure, I passed one of her former pediatricians in the hall. He asked what was up.

"Dr. Staub thinks Meghan may have a heart condition," I told him.

"Hmmm, I don't remember hearing anything," he replied.

I'll leave it at that.

Once the diagnosis of patent ductus arteriosus with pulmonary hypertension was made, we had to decide on a course of action. The luxury of time was taken away from us when Meghan developed respiratory syncytial virus (RSV), a common virus among the general population but one that could be deadly for a child with a congenital heart condition.

She was admitted immediately to Boston Children's Hospital, an amazing facility where children come from all over the world to get the latest and best treatment for some of the most rare and deadly diseases. Once there, I had a really good, long cry—a strange mixture of relief and fear flowing out of me with those tears. Although it was heart-breaking to have our child in the hospital, I sensed that we were finally in good hands and I could take a breath of my own, as the doctors took over and gave Meghan the care she needed.

This was the first opportunity for me to really begin to accept that Meghan was a very sick little girl. Because I had come to mistrust medical professionals after our struggle for an accurate diagnosis, it was really hard at first to let go and let the doctors take care of her. I prayed for guidance and one morning literally awoke with the conviction that we were all on the same team, the doctors, nurses, and Meghan's dad and I. We were "Team Meghan" and that was that!

Lesson One—Acceptance

> "What you resist persists."
> —C.G. Jung

The first few hours and days after the loss of a child is all about shock, which soon becomes intense grief and the constant reliving of the trauma. We need to keep moving to get things accomplished...things like funerals and memorial services. This is a time to just do our best, lean on others when there is an opportunity, and try to get rest whenever possible. This, for me, was a time of going through the motions, which was the best I could do. When all of the activity dies down, friends and family stop showing up, and we find ourselves alone with our new reality, it is time to get about the business of acceptance.

Whether it's the acceptance of a diagnosis, an addiction, the end of a relationship, or a job loss, this step is crucial to getting on the path back to happy.

Acceptance is a psychological relaxation into what is. It means we have reached a point of nonresistance. The struggle is over and it's time to sit in peaceful acceptance for a while to really feel what it's like. I have never fully appreciated the overused phrase "it is what it is" until I began thinking about the importance of acceptance. This phrase describes it perfectly. It is exactly what it is, so why not accept it? For a parent whose child has died, there is often reluctance to move toward acceptance as we (albeit irrationally) think it means we will lose connection with or somehow forget our child. Knowing that these feelings are normal is important for parents, as it is a bridge to the acceptance phase. Everything we are feeling is okay. There is no right way to do this grief thing.

The first step of the Alcoholics Anonymous (AA) Twelve-Step Program is to admit (aka "accept") that you are powerless over alcohol and that your life has become unmanageable. Why is this the first step? Makes so much sense, really. Acceptance creates a psychological shift that is necessary to begin the healing process. It's the first best place to start. It allows you to become part of a community with others, with a collective consciousness that is powerful and puts you in touch with those who have successfully gone before. The Twelve-Step Program is brilliant and has helped many with so much more than addiction because of its body, mind, and spirit approach.

For me, the acceptance of the fact that I had a daughter with a chronic, potentially life-threatening condition was difficult. I had to shed some tears, go through some angry moments, and revisit the clues that led us to solve the mystery of her illness. But the funny thing was that when I finally resigned myself to the reality of the situation, I found a certain peace there and a clarity that surprised me. I now knew where we stood, and there were some tangible steps that we could take to make things better. We could gather our team and strategize about what was in Meghan's best interest for her physical health, now and in the future. Little did I know at the time, the importance of learning acceptance and how

I would fall back on this awareness later on when the worst happened.

Acceptance can be tricky in some circumstances. For example, my friend Joe lost his job suddenly and fell into a deep depression, giving up all hope of finding something in his area of expertise. Attempts to find work that paid as well as his former job failed. It took him a long time to accept that perhaps it was time to think about looking for work in another field. As time went on, finally he was able to accept that his career as an independent contractor for the government was over. He was open to seeing that his life could be happier and even more fulfilling as a landscape designer, a skill he enjoyed learning, little by little, doing contract work for a friend.

Acceptance can take time. It requires sitting with the discomfort of whatever challenge is there and really observing our response to it. How many people do you know who have found love only after finally declaring that they didn't need another person in their lives to be truly happy? I can think of many! When my workout partner Jill's husband left her suddenly and without warning, she was in a state of shock for a while. She was devastated. She lost a lot of weight and wondered what in the world had just happened to her. After about a year of hoping to put the pieces of her broken marriage back together, she acknowledged to herself that it was over. Her husband was not coming back. Now she is happily dating her high school sweetheart and seems happier than I have seen her in a long time.

How do we know when we have reached a state of acceptance versus giving up or copping out? Acceptance brings us peace. It doesn't come overnight, but when it does, the sense that it is right and good is palpable and easy to recognize. If we don't feel that peace, we can be sure we are not there yet. Acceptance is the first rung of the ladder back up to happy. I encourage you to climb on up. It's a good thing!

Acceptance

Accept everything that comes your way as God-given. Pleasure, accept it. Pain, accept it. Profit, accept it. Loss, accept it. By accepting everything, the great benefit is you don't disturb your peace. You are always in peace. That is what we are looking for. That is what real yoga is. That is what real spiritual attainment is. That's what you call enlightenment. So learn to accept things. That doesn't mean that you shouldn't think of doing something, wanting to get something. It's better not to have any wants, but if you still want it, okay. Have your wants under one condition: the wants should be approved by the Higher Power. If you get it, all right, it was approved. If you don't get it, all right, it was disapproved. There is no harm in that kind of want.
Om Shanti, Shanti, Shanti
—Sri Swami Satchidananda, Founder of Integral Yoga

One of the podcasts that might be helpful as you begin this journey, *Back to Happy*, is "Lasting Transformation"(http://conniebowman.com/happyhealthyyou/2014/02/lasting-transformation/) with Dr. Abby Rosen. In this podcast, she talks about cultivating awareness of our patterns and choices as a means to self-acceptance and personal growth.

two

Good Days and Bad Days

Meghan had a tough go of it for the next several years. She would have some really great days and then some terribly hard days. That was the nature of her illness. I remember a young nurse in the early days after her diagnosis encouraging me to "not spoil her" because she needed to be obedient with the many doctors and procedures in her future. She also gave me a glimpse into her life with this disease. She said there would be times when we thought she was just fine, and the next minute she could be turning blue and almost lose consciousness as her sensitive little lungs would go into spasm.

I began to be hypersensitive to Meghan's needs. I was almost able to telepathically hear when she needed her oxygen (or "O2" as she called it). I think moms can relate to this as so many of us experience the classic "mother's intuition" that we've all heard about. This was my super power. I was able to somehow know, even when I was in another part of the house, that she needed me and her oxygen, which I would deliver to her ASAP. This hyper alert state was not so great for my own health, as you can imagine. I still had the anxiety attacks and now a real reason to be anxious.

One day, I was driving past a wellness center that I had been curious about for a while. It had a sign outside that said something about alternative healing. I decided to see what it was all about.

As I entered the building, I was greeted by a warm-hearted, middle-aged woman who listened to my story about Meghan and my panic attacks. She asked me if I would like to have a Reiki treatment. Having never heard of Reiki, but being very curious—also not wanting to be rude—I lay down fully clothed on her massage table for my first experience with energy healing.

From the moment I felt her hands gently graze the top of my head, I became calmer. By the end of the hour, I felt a little more like myself again. It was an amazing healing experience. I considered it a *God-thing* that I happened to walk into her office that day. It opened me to the real power of energy healing, which has stayed with me to this day.

Although I didn't have another Reiki treatment for decades, I felt so grateful to have been touched by this beautiful soul. It was part of my own healing, and it helped me learn to manage the stress that I was experiencing. Today, I too am a Reiki practitioner.

Meghan continued to have periods of health interspersed with hospital stays for colds that would develop into infections, each time requiring me to stay with her at the hospital. She also underwent a new (at the time) procedure; a clamshell occluder device was implanted into her heart that closed the troublesome hole just enough to release some of the pressure on her lungs. With every hospitalization or doctor visit, I was further impressed with the doctors and other medical professionals who dedicated their lives to working with critically ill children. Their expertise was impressive, but to witness their compassion firsthand, now that was inspiring.

One particular nurse would lovingly wash Meghan's hair and take the time to braid it in a beautiful French braid every day she was on duty. Meghan's first cardiologist shared a birthday with her, so he would chat with her about that and tell her she was his favorite because of it. Stories like these, which are too many to mention, fill my heart as I remember them.

Caroline, our second daughter, was born three years after Meghan and was a healthy, bright, cheerful baby who quickly became Meghan's shadow. I will always cherish those three years with my two beautiful little girls. I have vivid and fond memories of their sweet relationship—Meghan's protectiveness of her baby sister and Caroline's compassion for Meghan when she was in physical distress.

Meghan started her kindergarten year in relatively good health, and we were excited with her progress. It took some real convincing to get her into the local school, which didn't have a full-time nurse at the time—a requirement for a student who might need doses of oxygen on occasion. It was clear that the school officials were hesitant to accept a student with such special needs, but I felt Meghan needed to be there in the school with her neighborhood friends, living life as normally as possible. It was no problem delivering the oxygen tank to the school, but who was going to administer the O2 should she need it? Apparently I was, and so I spent the first week or so sitting in the school office keeping myself busy stuffing envelopes and doing other volunteer administrative tasks until they were able to have a nurse on staff.

Lesson Two—Connection to Spirit

"In all ways, acknowledge Him and He shall direct your paths."
—*Proverbs 3:6*

On a daily basis I was acutely aware that Meghan needed me. She needed me to be vigilant and responsive to her needs, should she require oxygen. She was also taking medication that needed to be dispensed daily.

I was now a new mom to another little girl who was thankfully healthy, strong, and energetic. My husband and I shared responsibilities for our family business. We had a house to take care of and the typical busy life that most young families experience.

A little stress is normal. The type of stress that comes with also caring for a seriously ill child can put a human over the edge and send him or her into fight or flight response, which I found myself in, as manifested by the frequent panic attacks I was having. I knew I had to get things in balance. I got a little taste of it during the Reiki session, but there was more work that needed to be done so that I could function healthfully and be there for my family.

I have always been a prayer. I prayed for my family and myself; I prayed for people in the world who were having hard times. Heck, I prayed for animals that died along the highway. In my early years, I think I prayed for two reasons primarily. I prayed to ask God for things that I wanted or to spare me from things that I feared. God was my reality, and

I believed that "He" was in charge and that I had very little say in most matters.

At this time in my life, with real life-and-death issues at stake, my prayers were more fervent, more passionate perhaps, and definitely more urgent. I needed God to hear me. I wanted my little girl healed and to live a long, happy, healthy life. I asked for that daily.

I also asked for my own healing. I needed to feel more peaceful. The discomfort of the anxious state was unbearable. What I found as I prayed more seriously and with feeling and love was a stronger connection to God or Spirit. When we pray, we open up a channel to God. Like a clear signal on a cell phone that gets better as we near the source of power, our connection to Spirit gets stronger the more we pray.

While prayer is talking to God, meditation is active listening to what God has to say. Meditation quiets the mind so that the important messages can come through. It is a practice that gets easier and easier over time. As I prayed and meditated, I began to get messages that gave clear direction about what I needed to do. I heeded those messages and things started to change. I encourage you to pray as often as you need to. Design your day so that it includes times of quiet where you can meditate and contemplate.

I started eating better, running, meditating regularly, and even journaling. Gradually the panic subsided, and I was able to be at peace with the situation and even to feel joy on occasion. I started to realize that if my days with my daughter were possibly going to be limited, I needed them to be the best they could be.

I started noticing small things to be grateful for. I had always been a grateful person, but stress can block even the most appreciative inclinations. I noticed that when I prayed prayers of thanks for little victories—like Meghan finishing her dinner without vomiting or having a great day without turning blue and needing her oxygen—it seemed as if more reasons to be grateful would show up. Small coincidences would happen to remind me that I was not alone. I felt sometimes as though hidden hands were guiding me.

Eventually faith replaced fear, and I was able to relax and enjoy life with my two precious little girls. It didn't happen overnight, but it did happen.

Now, I was raised with a Christian foundation, so that was naturally my go-to stress-relief system. Leaning on my faith helped me get more deeply connected to my higher power. This connection opened me to the insights and guidance for staying healthy during this stressful time.

The second step in the AA Twelve-Step Program is just this: *Get in touch with your higher power.* I cannot recommend this highly enough. It was the key to peace for me and really always has been. Find your own connection to God, Goddess, Spirit, Love, Goodness—whatever you choose to call it. Just find it, cultivate it, have faith in it and know it's got your back. It works. It just does. Try to be open to the healing that can come through finding and keeping sacred at all costs your relationship with the God of your understanding.

Once the connection to Spirit is made, then do your part to keep it strong. Meditate, eat well, get regular exercise, talk to people about what you are going through, and get good, quality therapy if necessary. The mind, body, and spirit must be in balance for us to function at our highest level and to just flat-out feel good. But for me, it all started with prayer.

Find quiet times during the day to have your own conversation with the God of your understanding. Open that conversation and keep it going for the rest of your life! Practice daily meditation (even for five minutes) to still the mind and open your heart and mind to receive guidance. This works and it's good!

Here's a Happy Healthy You! Podcast about meditation: http://conniebowman.com/happyhealthyyou/2013/04/meditation-with-scott-morgan/

three

Okay to Go

Despite her physical challenges, Meghan was a sweet, happy child. When her little sister Caroline was born, she showered her with love and affection. Meghan had just turned six when we took her to Children's Hospital to have a routine test to check the pressures in her lungs with some new medicines. It was to be a quick procedure, and she would be back in her kindergarten class the next day. No big deal. When they called my husband and me into the ICU after the procedure, it was to see if we could calm Meghan down as the nurses said she was agitated. When I saw her, I knew immediately there was something seriously wrong. Yes, she was agitated, but she was also struggling to breathe, and her coloring was dark blue. I tried to soothe and comfort her, but she coded on the table, and we were quickly ushered out of the room while the doctors and nurses worked to save her life.

The next two weeks were a blur. She was flown to Pittsburgh Children's Hospital, the only area facility that had a heart-lung machine called ECMO, which would keep her alive while we talked about heart transplants and other equally inconceivable things. I was not allowed to accompany Meghan, so I had to find the next flight out by commercial airline. Miraculously, my flight and Meghan's must have arrived at close to the same time because, when I hopped out of my cab, her ambulance was there. When they wheeled her out, I jumped onto the elevator reserved for patients heading to Emergency and rode with my daughter. Nobody said a word as I talked to my unconscious child who lay helpless on that gurney.

I was in the first trimester of pregnancy with my son, Bobby, at that time and had my first ultrasound while Meghan was in that hospital. Thankfully, Bobby looked to be healthy and was growing well, so that was a relief and a blessing. Blessings were few and far between, but I found them to be like hidden gems during my otherwise stressful days in that ICU. A particular salad stands out as being ultra-tasty, a soft pillow under my head for a nap in the visitor's lounge felt like heaven, and visits from friends and family kept our spirits bolstered. Although her dad and I did take breaks from being at her side, our time spent out of the hospital was limited to quick meals or walks for fresh air but did wonders for our sanity and perspective.

Meghan was kept sedated while hooked to ECMO. Because the machine was oxygenating her blood, she looked deceivably good to us. So on May 5, 1991, the day the doctors came to us and told us it was time to let her go, we were devastated. I prayed about it and felt this peace come over me and knew in my heart they were right. She had been through so much, and her little body had fought hard to stay with us, but now we needed to tell her that it was all right to go. Thank God for the angel nurse who suggested I whisper to Meghan that it was "okay to go." When the time came, that's what I did. I gently pulled the curtains around her bed for privacy, and I told her it was okay and that I would see her when I got there. Soon after that, she died peacefully in that hospital bed, her dad and me at her side.

Lesson Three—Grace and Gratitude

"If the only prayer you said was thank you, that would be enough."
—Meister Eckhart

I call this powerful duo G-Squared. Grace and gratitude were two important facets of the journey for me. Grace is the presence of God showing up when most needed in the form of people, unexplainable poise during challenging times, inspiration and intuition, and so many other ways. Gratitude is the appreciation of the good that is present in any moment. Both grace and gratitude require a certain amount of awareness and an openness to receive.

During times of high stress and trauma, remembering to lean on others is so very important. If you are a "pull yourself up by your bootstraps" kind of person, now is the time to let that go. Allow the love of others to bolster you and give you the strength you need to carry on. There are times when we will be unable to hold it together, but our loved ones can. It's okay to let it out and cry and sob and express whatever emotions are coming up. Let those who love you support you. Don't worry; you'll get a chance to pay them back, and you will be all the more glad for the opportunity. I recall that period in my life with wonder, in that my husband and I never "lost it" at the same time. I would cry on his shoulder, and he would be there to console me. Later, he would break down, and I would hold him. Noticing the pure grace that is available at these times builds faith and helps us to know for sure we are never really alone.

Gratitude for the smallest, simplest things keeps us positive during the direst of circumstances and helps raise our spirits and the spirits of those around us. Gratitude has a psychological and physiological effect on the body-mind and helps our whole system to function at equilibrium. Many people keep a running gratitude journal to chronicle the small and large things that come into their lives. Notice and appreciate even the tiniest kind gesture, beautiful sky, or fleeting happy thought, and they will multiply. I promise.

Jot down the small gifts that come into your life even during times of high stress. Give thanks for these blessings, however small. Practicing gratitude will begin to shift things for you, little by little. Remember, though, it's a marathon and not a sprint. Gratitude is a practice. Not only is gratitude good for you, gratitude is contagious and makes the world a happier place to live. Build those gratitude muscles by noting everything you are grateful for and watch the miracles start to happen!

Oh, and thank *you* for reading this! ☺

Here's a podcast about someone who turned gratitude into a business. Now that's a solid gratitude practice!!! http://conniebowman.com/happyhealthyyou/2013/08/sweet-gratitude/

four

A New Life

Meghan's death shook my foundation out from under me. From that day on, my life would never be the same. I had always wanted to have kids, lots of them. Meghan was my first. I loved being her mommy; and now she was gone.

In the early hours after her death, something took over, and I went into planning mode, deciding whom I needed to call and what needed to be arranged. A certain adrenaline rush kicked in that I really couldn't explain, and I got through those days of planning her funeral service and burial with energy that came from reserves I had stored up somewhere. Things went smoothly, and many great people were there for us in those early days, including family, friends, and clergy.

I think that when these shocking and life-changing things happen in our lives—hard things like death, diagnosis, divorce—we are forced to stop...to just stop. And once all that had been required of me was essentially done, that's what happened. I just stopped. I stopped to look at what had just unfolded in my life and the life of my family over that past few weeks. I stopped to reflect on what Meghan had been through and I did a lot of reliving her ordeal as though I could take some of it away by reliving it myself. I stopped to try and figure out how my life could possibly be lived without this precious little girl who had been my primary focus for the six years of her short life. I stopped and I cried. And I cried and I cried some more. I would get in my car all alone and, windows rolled up so no one could hear, I would scream and sob as loudly as I could. I cried in the shower, letting the warm water soothe me and muffle the sound. Sometimes grief would overtake me at the strangest and most unpredictable times, and I would just have to remove myself from whatever social situation I was in and find a private place to let go and release.

One day it came to me that I needed to reread Elizabeth Kubler-Ross's book *On Death and Dying* to familiarize myself with the stages of grief. I had read it in college and knew there was some kind of a plan there for getting through the quagmire of grief. I mentioned this to a friend, and within a couple of hours, he showed up at our house with that book! "Amazing grace," indeed!

I studied the book and tried to move through each of the phases of grief in as academic and systematic way as was possible. The stages are denial, anger, bargaining, depression, and acceptance. I recognized in myself many of the stages, but they weren't linear and they weren't ordered as Dr. Kubler-Ross orders them. The material in the book was good in theory, and it did give me a framework to start the healing process, but for me, it was just that—a framework. I began to develop my own ways of coping and moving back toward wholeness, but not before I took the next most important step.

Lesson Four—Time Out

"To weep is to make less the depth of grief."
—*William Shakespeare*

When life throws us curveballs, sometimes the only choice we have is to stop and take the time to feel the effect of the unhittable pitch. We feel angry, sad, out of control, and lost. We need time to process these feelings in the natural way we were designed to do. We need to cry, stamp our feet, talk about our fears for the future and our sense of hopelessness. This is okay! This is good, healthy stuff, and it takes time. We need to give ourselves permission to take a break and honor the process of healing that is taking place, whether it means, taking a leave of absence from work, asking for help with child care, allowing others to cook or even clean for us, or bowing out of volunteer and other obligations for as long as it feels right. Time does heal, but not if we don't let it!

During this time, it is good to journal, talk to trusted friends or professionals, and, for goodness sake, cry as much as you feel like. If you have children who see you express-ing emotion, simply explain to them that "Mommy is sad about..." or "Daddy is crying because he feels sad and that's okay. It's good to cry when you feel sad."

I cannot emphasize enough how crucial this allowance of feelings and emotions is to the early healing process. Give yourself permission to release and let go by allowing the feelings you are experiencing. It is our right and our duty to ourselves to do this. Take the time you need to stop and feel so that you can heal. Shedding tears helps us to process and move the toxic, stress-induced chemicals from our body.

According to Dr. William Frey from the Ramsey Medical Center in Minneapolis, "Emotional tears contain stress hormones, which get excreted from the body through crying." Frey studied the composition of tears and found that they actually do facilitate the removal of toxins and hormones that accumulate in our bodies as a result of stress.

Time spent sitting with the intense feelings of these early days is time well spent. It will pay off by helping you move forward on your healthy healing journey.

Max Strom's book *There is No App for Happiness* was super helpful for me, and he was kind enough to let me interview him for the *Happy Healthy You!* podcast. Here's the link: http://conniebowman.com/happyhealthyyou/2013/08/there-is-no-app-for-happiness/

five

A Day at a Time

Grief has no timetable, save the one we allow ourselves, and this process for me was dragging on. I took each day one at a time and dealt with the emotions that would arise almost spontaneously and at random times. One practical thing that I found helpful was to make a list of even the simplest tasks that I wanted to get done on a given day. I'd list everything from brushing my teeth to buying Caroline a new pair of shoes. I cut myself an awful lot of slack with the tougher assignments I gave myself and settled on accomplishing smaller, more manageable ones in the beginning.

I wondered, after a few months, when things would start to look up and I would feel even just a little better. I wasn't asking for the world, just a little breakthrough so that I could enjoy life, my marriage, and my living children for small periods of time without frequent crying jags and those now-familiar feelings of hopelessness.

One day when I had just really had enough, I heard something very clearly. "Surrender," the voice said. I'll never forget that day because something compelled me to literally get down on my knees in my living room and pray a serious and committed prayer of surrender. I told God that

I could not do this on my own and that I surrendered this missing of Meghan to Him/Her. I did a sort of mental and spiritual washing of the hands. Instead of continuing to try controlling my own heart and mind, I opened myself to the grace that I hoped would be there to help.

There is the saying that "we make plans and God laughs." Broadway actress and podcast guest Desi Oakley learned once just how true that is. Her life was going along perfectly, or so it seemed. She was engaged to be married to a handsome guy, and her acting career was moving along beautifully. Wedding plans were under way and going well. One day out of the blue, her fiancé announced that he was breaking off the engagement. Her world was rocked, and Desi was left heartbroken and inconsolable. With her strong faith, Desi knew surrender was her only option. She turned it all over to God, and her healing took on an almost magical quality.

Before long, Desi had booked a national tour, she was inspired to write music about her experience and produced an album, and, best of all, she attracted a new love—a great guy who shares her spiritual and personal values.

As it was for Desi, the act of surrendering my problems to my higher power or God was a distinct turning point for me. Although I did not have a spontaneous healing right then and there, I felt a marked sense of hope for the future. I started to slowly detect signs of getting back to happy at this time. I would have fleeting moments of joy that would be sustained for longer and longer periods. It was as though I had to relearn how to feel joy after the trauma of losing Meghan. Although it was happening, it was happening slowly and I had to be okay with that.

Lesson Five—Surrender

"The greatness of a man's power is the measure of his surrender."
—William Booth

Surrender was a pivotal point for me and it can be for you too. The Serenity Prayer is a beautiful prayer of surrender: "God grant me the serenity to accept the things I cannot change, the courage to change the things I can, and the wisdom to know the difference."

When we accept that we are not in control of the bigger picture and just take care of our end of the bargain, which is to live every day in alignment with our soul, now that's a big-time game-changer. Things start to fall into place and life takes on a whole new framework. We are free of the responsibility that was never ours to begin with.

What does surrender mean from a practical standpoint? It means not forcing things that don't happen easily. It means not planning so far in advance that we are not leaving room for opportunities that want to come into our lives. It means trusting our intuition or our "still small voice" when things don't feel right or when they feel completely awesome. All of this surrendering takes a bit of practice, so don't expect to change overnight. Little by little, your life will seem more magical with surrender. Everything will be less of a struggle. Your life will be pointing you in the direction of—dare I say it—happy!

Surrender was huge for me. When I allowed God to take the reins and let things unfold organically, my world shifted and happiness became a real possibility. Little "miracles" started to happen in my life, seemingly out of nowhere, and continue to do so.

Here's the podcast with actress Desi Oakley. I think you will love her music: http://conniebowman.com/happyhealthyyou/2014/06/dont-look-back/

six

Dreams

After the surrender came the miracles. There were so many I can barely recall all of them, but I will tell you about two. How I wish I had written them all down at the time I experienced them. Maybe you could!

Every parent who loses a child longs to dream about him or her. In the early days after Meghan's death, I wasn't able to dream about her. Emotions were still running high then, and I think the absence of dreams during that time is our psyche's way to protect us. One morning, however, I woke up after a profoundly real dream. In the dream, Meghan told me that she couldn't be happy until I was happy. I distinctly remembered her telling me that in those exact words. Within a week of my having that dream, my sister-in-law sent me a copy of a newspaper article that she felt compelled to share with me. It was illustrated by a drawing of several little angels marching in heaven—all of them carrying lighted candles. One angel's candle kept going out. When another angel asked her why her candle kept going out, she replied, "My mother's tears keep putting it out." Well, that was all I needed. I knew then it was time to start getting serious about my own happiness, if not for me and my family, then for Meghan. Only after that dream was I able to get on about the business of being a mom to my two living children with a renewed sense of purpose.

Not long after my son, Bobby was born, my dear, dear former high school drama teacher called to tell me she was working with a community theater group, and she invited me to audition for their next play. I had been active in theater productions in high school and college, but after graduation, I let a lot of my acting pursuits fall by the wayside. In fact, I'd taken a job in advertising and public relations, which left no time for my theater pursuits. There was always a lot of joy associated with acting and performing for me, especially in musical theater. I was excited about the possibility of getting involved again.

I ended up working with that theater group for many years, and my family became involved too, with Caroline joining me on stage, and my husband in the orchestra pit. This was not something that I pursued but rather something that came to me. Now I owe my acting career to that one phone call, and my daughter's acting career as well. Had I not been looking for the miracles and open to receive them, I possibly never would have answered.

Lesson Six—Bliss

> *"Follow Your Bliss."*
> —Joseph Campbell

There is magic that happens when we follow our hearts, our passions, and our bliss. If there was one thing that was clear to me after going through this great loss, it was that life is precious and short, and we should live it as if we mean it!

American anthropologist Joseph Campbell talks about following our bliss and the "hidden hands" that appear to help when we need them. Doors open where they were previously closed to us. Opportunities appear out of the blue.

We have to pay attention, though. That is our work. When these opportunities arise, we must see them as just that and say a big fat *yes*! to them. This is a big sticking point for many, I think. If I had paused for a moment when my former teacher called me to audition, the chance to perform again may have passed me by. My advice for this phase is to say yes, and then figure out how to do it. That very first yes has turned into a flourishing acting career for me. I never could have dreamed up the fun and exciting opportunities that have come along since then.

My friend and colleague Susan took a voice-over gig that seemed to be a run-of-the-mill job, but she had been following her bliss and heeding the signs and that job turned into one that made her voice one of the most familiar voices to all of us. Susan Bennett is the voice of iPhone's Siri. Her podcast (link below) is interesting and inspiring because it reminds us to follow through with what makes us tingle, as it could very well lead us down a path to our destiny.

I love Donna Faulds's poetry. She does yoga and says the poems just spontaneously arise from her practice. Here's one of her poems that I particularly love:

"Consider the Lilies"

Consider the lilies,
how they use their
precious blooming to
share beauty with
this world. You, too,
are given life to cultivate your gifts
and let them lift you
out of fear and doubt.
A vast garden of love
is all around you now
if you can see beyond
the tangled weeds
to the mystery and
radiance beneath.

From Donna Faulds's *Breath of Joy*

Here's Susan Bennett's (voice of Siri) podcast: http://conniebowman.com/happyhealthyyou/2014/03/dream-jobs/

Here's another podcast with Serena Dyer about the book she co-wrote with her dad, Wayne Dyer, *Don't Die with Your Music Still in You:*
http://conniebowman.com/happyhealthyyou/2014/08/dont-die-with-your-music-still-in-you/

seven

Glimpses of Joy

As life went on for me, slowly, slowly things started to shift. Joy came back to me at the strangest of times. With it came an acute awareness of its presence, which further magnified its pleasure. I can only imagine someone who has been in deep depression waking up one day to feel a sliver of hope for happiness. When in the thick of it, we cannot even fathom what that sliver would be like, but when it arrives, it is like a long lost love who has come back to us. We want to hold onto it, never let it go. But joy is fleeting on the best of days. The most we can do is recognize it and be grateful for its appearance.

When these small glimpses of joy and peace started arriving more regularly, I looked for ways to sustain the feeling. Always an exerciser, I knew that running and swimming were easy ways to raise the endorphin (feel-good hormones) levels in my body, so I made sure to get lots of exercise.

I began to incorporate yoga into my life. Yoga is all about awareness and being present to what is in our lives. The physical practice that is yoga strengthened my body, and the mental practice began to train my mind to be still, even in times of stress. When you are holding a tough yoga pose and the instructor says to breathe, sometimes you want to shout expletives at her. But, truly, yoga for me has been the best workshop for learning to stay with something even if it is highly uncomfortable. There is a balance in yoga of effort and surrender that is really beautiful and translates into life for me. Also, the breathing techniques reminded me to use the breath as a tool for relaxation and stress relief on a more regular basis.

I started meditating back when I was experiencing the panic attacks in my twenties. It helped center me and put me in touch with my inner life in a much deeper way. (Yoga also includes a short meditative practice.) I started going deeper and deeper and being able to access that calm centered space much more easily with practice. Like yoga, meditation is a practice but one that pays off with greater calm and lowered blood pressure. It's a great attitude adjuster.

As previously mentioned, meditation opens up the channel to more clearly hear God and prayer is talking to God. Both are important for an ongoing dialogue. My prayer life has always been rather loud and suppliant, but I now found myself bringing in prayers of gratitude for every little blessing that came along. That very act seemed to multiply the blessings. I noticed that the more I gave thanks, the more blessings would come my way.

Lesson Seven—Balance

> *"Life is a balance of holding on and letting go."*
> —*Rumi*

Part of the journey *Back to Happy* involves finding balance in mind, body, and spirit. Of course, a balanced, healthy diet with lots of fruits and vegetables is important; we all know that. Not only is good nutrition great for the body, but it also makes us feel better to eat a light diet of good, organic food. Good food makes us feel better in the body that we live in.

Exercise has always been part of my daily routine. I have been a runner and a swimmer for years and take classes at the gym as well. I play tennis in the spring and summer. When I added yoga to the mix several years ago, a whole new world of mind/body awareness opened up for me.

Yoga is an amazing practice that creates an opportunity for us to be present in our bodies, build strength and patience with ourselves, and cultivate stillness, which makes meditation an even more enjoyable practice. Meditation is a practice that clears the mind of the clutter that our daily lives leave laying around. In the stillness, we are able to reduce stress and, with time, cultivate an opening to Spirit, God, the Universe, whatever you choose to call the higher power in your life. Yoga and meditation have been essential to this healing journey and have brought me tremendous peace.

There are many other things to try. Tai Chi and/or Qi Gong are both slow, meditative practices that move the body in ways that open up energy channels and restore balance. I keep the tools from healing modalities like acupuncture, Reiki, massage, reflexology, chiropractic, and others in my toolbox to use when I am feeling out of balance.

Reading sacred texts and spiritual books has also helped me. Find the authors and teachers that speak to your soul. Revisit the religion of your childhood if you have left that behind. I have found a richness and a depth and also great comfort in many of the ancient religions. Visiting sacred sites and sitting in the energy where many have prayed before is amazing. I recall visiting St. Patrick's Cathedral in New York City and seeing the statue *Pieta* for the first time. I was in tears as I stood there in front of that beautiful statue. I experienced the same feeling of awe when visiting the majesty and breathtaking splendor of God's spectacular creations in Sedona, Arizona.

If you want to create a ritual around special dates that remind you of your loved one, I suggest you follow your intuition. Decide how much effort you want to invest. Maybe it's as simple as releasing a balloon on a birthday or visiting a favorite spot in nature. Light a candle in honor of your beloved or revisit old photographs that bring back good memories. Whatever it is, make sure it feels right to you and the rest of the family. It can be a beautiful way to pay tribute and healing for you as well.

Finally, I suggest that you create a sacred space of your own in your home where you can pray and meditate and even journal, if you wish. Perhaps you could include an altar where you place small, sacred objects, a candle, and/or a photo of a loved one or saint. Designating a space for worship and contemplation brings the energy of God into your home and reminds you to pay a visit. Your private sanctuary will quickly become your favorite part of your home.

Here's a link to a video I produced that talks about creating your own sacred space: https://www.youtube.com/watch?v=bH2hECLn5Qk&list=UUP3KZ7i2VHstZ0iOcdQykYA

And another with a terrific yoga practice you can do at home: https://www.youtube.com/watch?v=hZXqDkAH_2I &list=TLqoRasBrNcCgNfQVz2YKdRqb4ly5dfXKk

Here's the *Happy Healthy You!* podcast about chiropractic: http://conniebowman.com/happyhealthyyou/2014/05/ boning-up-on-chiropractic-sorry/

eight

Compassion

As happiness started to fill in the cracks and crevices of my life, I began to have opportunities to reach out to others and discovered a newfound and deep compassion within myself. I related empathically to those who were on their individual healing journeys and found myself drawn to their stories and lives.

I was now able to listen and share with other parents who had lost children, where before my pain was just too great and I had nothing to offer them. We cannot give what we do not have ourselves. The good inner work I had been doing had replenished and strengthened me so that I could offer myself to others.

I had a nice career going as an actress and voice-over talent. I had a great studio for producing my commercials and narrations. About that time, I started to think about producing a *podcast.* Suddenly podcasts were showing up everywhere on my radar screen. I started thinking they might be something I could do, and maybe—just maybe—podcasting was to be part of my healing ministry. I pondered this and searched my heart and soul for a potential subject matter, should I decide to create a podcast program. One day a friend commented that I was healthy and fit and that that inspired her. Okay, I thought, maybe this is a place to start. I truly believe that taking that first step is the most important part of any journey. We don't need all of the answers at once, and everything does not have to be perfectly in place to get started on our missions. When we step out in faith, doors start to open. So I took the first step, gave my podcast a nice, bright, and sunny name, and created a logo. And that day, *Happy Healthy You!* the podcast was born.

This would be my forum for expressing compassion for others and reaching out with messages of hope and health and healing. I really do believe that for us to be happy—truly happy–we need to find a balance of mind, body, and spirit and that is the mission of *Happy Healthy You!*

I have recorded many great conversations with people who are following their bliss, living lives of service, and working in healing fields. The podcast has become a passion project and an expression of my creativity and my spirit. In many ways, I felt as though it was the final part of this healing journey.

Then I was asked to officiate at a memorial service. This is one of those *God-things* that just came in seemingly out of the blue. I had to say yes to it because it was just so out of the ordinary. The priest at my church asked me to take over for her at a funeral that she was unable to attend because of a prior commitment. Although I hesitated at first, not feeling worthy of such a challenge, I agreed to give it a go, trusting that all was in divine order. She walked me though all of the details and made me feel that I was in every way capable to taking on this task. She told me that the most important part of this job would be guiding the family through the service and helping them through the experience of memorializing and grieving for their loved one. I was all over this. I said, "Thank you, God." Maybe this was the final chapter of healing from grief. This was a chance to help others with my own experience and seal the deal for myself as well. I was ready.

The service was beautiful, the family was gracious and grateful, and the honor that it was to fulfill that duty was beyond profound. I thought I would be nervous, but thankfully, I was not. I felt a holy presence with us all that day, making things run smoothly. It was a sacred opportunity that I am more than grateful for having been able to experience.

Compassion for others deepens when we go through the grief journey, and it is a gift to be shared. Living in the space of compassion and love for others almost mystically brings in opportunities to minister to those in need. People mysteriously cross our paths. They may just need a word or two of encouragement from us. Again, I suggest that you be open to those who may need your love and wisdom on any given day. You've been through a lot. You have much to share. When we share, we close the circle of healing for ourselves, and we are able to move forward to an awakened life of peace and joy.

Lesson Eight—Reaching Out

"A new command I give you: Love one another. As I have loved you, so you must love one another. By this everyone will know that you are my disciples, if you love one another."
—*John 13:34–35*

Having compassion for others is an important aspect of being human. Compassion is defined as a sense of shared suffering, most often combined with a desire to alleviate or reduce the suffering of another—to show special kindness to those who suffer. Compassion essentially arises through empathy and is often characterized through actions wherein a person acting with compassion will seek to aid those they feel compassion for. The Dalai Lama says, "If you want others to be happy, practice compassion. If you want to be happy, practice compassion."

As I learned at an early Compassionate Friends meeting soon after Meghan's death, the final stage that we all want to reach is that of helping another in his or her grief. While sitting in that meeting, I was overwhelmed by the stories others told about their own losses. It was too much for me to take in at the time. I was dealing with my own raw grief and could not bear to hear that anyone else had similar or more tragic stories than my own. One family at the meeting had lost two children, which was beyond my comprehension at the time.

But one thing stuck with me from that meeting and that was the need to reach out to others when the time was right. This, they told us, would not only help the person we were reaching out to, but it would help us with our own healing. From that night on, it became my mission to get to that place. Whatever I needed to do to get there, I was willing to try. My route took lots of side roads—proverbial roads less travelled—but eventually I got there.

With my podcast, *Happy Healthy You!,* I have been promoting many groups and individuals who are doing great work in the world. I have met so many inspiring people whose work is helping those less fortunate or those who need healing. The teachers and authors I have interviewed truly have a passion for what they do and a mission to help others with their gifts.

When Fred Gabler died in the attacks on the World Trade Center on 9/11, his friends and family were devastated. Fred was so beloved. He worked for Cantor Fitzgerald, the financial firm that lost the most employees on that sad day. One evening, I was in New York City in a hotel restaurant waiting for my daughter to come out of the show she was working on, *Kinky Boots*, when I struck up a conversation about running shoes, of all things, with two women sitting at the table next to me. There was something about these two that drew us together, but I couldn't put my finger on it at the time. We kept in touch over email and I came to find out that one of the women was Edie Lutnick, cofounder and president of the Cantor Fitzgerald Relief Fund, which was established to help families of victims who perished on 9/11. The other was Jolie Gabler, sister of Fred Gabler, who also happened to be Billy Crystal's stage manager. When Fred died, grief-stricken friends and family got together to establish the Fred Gabler Helping Hands Camp Fund, in honor of Fred's life. This camp fund has helped many children who would be unable to afford summer camp and have the experience that Fred had so loved during his childhood.

The Fred Gabler Helping Hands Camp Fund is now supported by the Broadway community, ensuring that Fred's life will be remembered and many children will benefit. Fred, like the thousands of others who died on that day, was loved dearly. Creating a memorial like this is just one way of reaching out to others. The healing potential is greatly multiplied when we come together in love to help others.

The act of helping others has a healing effect that is most miraculous. According to Mark Snyder, psychologist and head of the Center for the Study of the Individual and Society at the University of Minnesota, "People who volunteer tend to have higher self-esteem, psychological well-being, and happiness." He says, "All of these things go up as their feelings of social connectedness goes up, which in reality, it does. It also improves their health and even their longevity."

When Todd Nigro lost his six-year-old daughter Ellie to a tragic accident, he took on the task of helping others who were going through the same sort of grieving process he was. He, along with his wife, started Ellie's Way, a nonprofit that reaches out to families affected by the death of a child. Ellie's Way sends out care packages and ministers to many of the grieving, just as people did for Todd and his family after Ellie died. Todd appreciates the value of giving back, and the many people who have benefitted from his generosity are undoubtedly inspired by him to pass it on as well.

You can find your own way to reach out. Perhaps it has something to do with your wound, perhaps not. The gesture of reaching out and helping another human in his or her time of need is healing. It is love personified. Be a human angel. Don't think too much about the details. Just help wherever you see a need and things will miraculously fall into place for you. I would love to hear your stories, so please let me know how it goes.

Helping another, I learned, is the final stage of healing. It brings us full circle. Once we have learned this and all the other lessons, I believe we will not have to relearn them.

(Insert sigh of relief here.) So it pays to get them down as best we can.

Finally, and most importantly, love yourself. Be gentle with yourself, and respect your own individual healing process. Volunteer your love when you are ready. Everyone is remarkably and miraculously different and must follow his or her own guidance. There is no set timetable here. Trust the process. Trust your higher power. Trust your inner voice until it gets louder and stronger and leads you victoriously down that path *Back to Happy*.

Here's Fred Gabler's podcast: http://conniebowman.com/happyhealthyyou/2014/04/giving-back-is-a-beautiful-thing/

And my interview with Todd Nigro from Ellie's Way: http://conniebowman.com/happyhealthyyou/2013/12/life-after-loss/

And another podcast about the importance of compassion: http://conniebowman.com/happyhealthyyou/2014/10/compassion-is-cool/

nine

Happy Heroes

Getting *Back to Happy* is a noble journey that we all must take at some time. In many ways it's the hero's journey that Joseph Campbell writes about. It requires courage to feel deeply, look closely at our lives, and pay attention to our thoughts. If we accept the call, we must leave behind old ways of thinking and move forward into new and uncharted territory. We have been tested and now must make the decision to keep going, though at times we may not see the road before us. The promise of rebirth is there if we persevere.

According to Campbell, the "hero" has an opportunity to be transformed by his or her journey. I like this idea personally. If we have to go through something difficult, it's nice to think we might have some reward at the end. Losing my daughter was the hardest thing I could imagine. I never felt like much of a hero while I was grieving her loss, but perhaps I am. Perhaps we all are.

Many of you have or will go through equally difficult experiences in your life. It is my hope that this little book will help you ride the waves more smoothly with some of the tools I have suggested in the Lessons sections.

The final lesson may be difficult to think about but hey, what is difficult anymore, right? We may not even be conscious of our fear of death, and this could be a problem. Facing our own mortality requires courage and the ability to let go of our cultural proclivity to subdue our fears of death with unhealthy distractions like alcohol, drugs, food, shopping and gambling to name but a few. According to Lisa Firestone, Ph.D., "Our fears of mortality can leave us with an urge to retreat from life, to live less fully as a means of reducing the pain of our demise or the scope of what we would lose. The anxiety we feel may motivate us to give up the things that connect us to our physical selves, our sexuality, our bodily desires, or our bodies themselves. Yet this knowledge has the power to do just the opposite, to inspire us to live life full steam ahead, pursuing our most meaningful goals, staying close to our loved ones, and living with integrity, self-esteem, and purpose."

Well, there you go. Who'd have thought that facing our own death could lead to happiness? My daughter Caroline found her own way to deal with the death of her sister. One day, several months after Meghan died, I walked into our playroom to find Caroline and her friend playing dead. They would take turns lying on the floor. One person would be "dead" and the other would stand over her crying. I watched for several moments deliberating whether to interrupt or let the scene play out. I let them continue with their play-acting, and after a short while, they finished and went on to play something else. This went on for only a few months before they grew tired of it. I am grateful forever to Caroline's friend Alicia for being her scene partner and helping my daughter process her grief in her own way. If you're wondering, today Caroline is a happy, healthy young woman who will play the lead role of Elphaba in the hit Broadway musical *Wicked* as this book goes to press. Umm, grace? Yes, please. Thank you.

Recently I was cast in a film where I played a dying woman sad to leave her husband and daughter. The character I played allowed me to explore the reality of my own death and come to some peace with it. Although challenging at times, I was truly grateful for this opportunity.

You are the hero or heroine in your own life. Give yourself permission to let your unique personal story play itself out. Embrace what comes along with acceptance and love. Be grateful for everything and you *will* find joy again.

Lesson Nine—Peace with Death

"I knew that was really the only purpose of life: to be our self, live our truth, and be the love that we are."
—Anita Moorjani

Death is the biggie. It's probably the basis of all human fears. We don't really know what happens when we die. Our culture has created such fearful images around death it's no wonder we are scared, literally to death!

Making peace with the inevitability of death is probably our most important spiritual pursuit. Finding a sense of peace around death frees us to live our lives largely and with great love.

For those who fear death, the masters suggest we take a trip in our imaginations into our own possible death. Facing it head-on is not for the faint of heart, but it can be a healing journey like no other. Explore your own mortality in meditation and see what arises.You may find that the fears you have been holding onto are just thoughts that have been influenced by the culture. Maybe they could be released.

Read firsthand accounts of near-death experiences like Anita Moorjani's in her book *Dying to be Me* where she tells about her journey to the afterlife and back. Her story is inspiring in so many ways. The peace that she experienced while out of her body was extraordinary.

Working with an organization like hospice that helps the dying transition is another awesome opportunity to work through personal fears around death. There is even a college-level course on thanatology, which is the scientific study of death, including changes that occur in the body during the dying process as well as psychological experiences of those in transition.

Simply sitting with someone in the final phases of their life is an honor and a privilege and one that can open us further to the mysteries of life and death.

In closing this book, I would like to share my personal takeaway from the experience of losing a child, grieving her loss, and finding joy once again. I have come to the conclusion that love is all there is, ever was, and will be. Throughout this whole experience, as painful as it was, I was surrounded by love at all times. Of course, it is easy to see in retrospect. When I look back, I can plainly see that I was protected, guided, and loved from well before Meghan was born. I continue to feel guided, protected, and loved in a more profound way today, and I try to live my life with that awareness-so much so that I depend on God for small things like parking spaces and big things like inspiration for this book! She never disappoints. I always get exactly what I need, not necessarily what I want, but that's *all right*.

God is love. Love is all there is, and it never ends. This is the lesson of my lifetime.

So thank you, God.

And thank you, Meg.

"The Ship"

What is dying?
I am standing on the seashore.
A ship sails to the morning breeze and starts for the ocean.
She is an object, and I stand watching her
till at last she fades from the horizon.
And someone at my side says, "She is gone!" Gone where?
Gone from my sight, that is all.
She is just as large in the masts,
hull and spars as she was when I saw her.
And just as able to bear her load of living freight to its destination.
The diminished size and total loss of sight is in me, not in her.
And just at the moment when someone at my side says, "She is gone,"
there are others who are watching her coming.

And other voices take up a glad shout,
"There she comes"—and that is dying.

By Charles Henry Brent

And here is our podcast about making peace with death from the people at the International Association of Near-Death Studies: http://conniebowman.com/happyhealthyyou/2013/11/what-a-way-to-go/

Helpful Books, Links, Prayers and Other Stuff

For more of the *Happy Healthy You!* podcasts:
www.conniebowman.com/happyhealthyyou/

Contact information for The Compassionate Friends, a grief support organization:
http://www.compassionatefriends.org/Find_Support.aspx

Contact information for Grief Share:
http://www.griefshare.org

Favorite prayer: The Lord's Prayer, Matthew 6:9-13
Jesus himself told us to pray this prayer so...

Our Father who art in heaven
Hallowed be Thy name
Thy kingdom come.
Thy will be done.
On Earth as it is in heaven.
Give us this day our daily bread.

And forgive us our trespasses
As we forgive those who trespass against us.
And lead us not into temptation.
But deliver us from evil.
For thine is the kingdom
And the power and the glory.
Forever. Amen

Another good one:
The Serenity Prayer is the common name for a prayer authored by the American theologian Reinhold Niebuhr (1892–1971). It has been adopted by Alcoholics Anonymous and other twelve-step programs. The best-known form is:

God, grant me the serenity to accept the things I cannot change,
the courage to change the things I can,
and the wisdom to know the difference.

The Power of Now by Eckhart Tolle

Autobiography of a Yogi by Paramahansa Yogananda

Letters of the Scattered Brotherhood by Mary Strong

Favorite nutrition book: *Eat to Live* by Joel Furman, MD

Anything written by Anne Lamott

Any poetry by Rumi or Mary Oliver

My favorite online yoga video:

https://www.youtube.com/watch?v=G6XqCI7IbvE&list=T
LL0ThptkC60GP9wSqTai2Hvl0m-l8P_vl

Film that made a big impact on my diet: *Forks Over Knives*

This is the website: http://www.forksoverknives.com/
the-film/

And the film that helps me believe peace on Earth is possible if we just start with ourselves: *I Am* by director Tom Shadyac

Acknowledgments

I want to thank God for the inspiration to write. I know I asked you many times, "What exactly are we doing here?" but I know you see the bigger picture and *I do* trust you. I also thank my guides who are always with me gently nudging, sometimes pushing, and oftentimes screaming in my ear until I finally listen. To my loving team, I say, sorry I have been so stubborn.

To my sweet Meghan, I know you are always with me. I thank you for coming into my life to wake me up. You are the reason for this book and for so many things. Your sweetness opened my heart from the moment you were born, probably before. Your courage inspires me still. I'm sure we have been together in many other lifetimes. Oh how we will rejoice when we are together again!

To my family here on Earth, Rob, Caroline, Bobby, Mom, Dad, Sally, John and all the others, thank you for playing your roles so perfectly in this drama we call *life*. Your love and support has meant everything. I love you. I bless you. I just think you are the cat's pajamas.

Author Biography

Connie Bowman is an actress, voice-over talent, and pro-
ducer of the podcast *Happy Healthy You!* She has performed
in films, television, and in the theater. She lives in a state of
awe and wonder most of the time with her cute husband,
Rob. They have three children—Meghan (who is in heaven),
Caroline, and Bobby. *Back to Happy* is her first book. For more
information, visit her website at www.conniebowman.com.

Photo credit: Joe Henson Photography

Made in the USA
Middletown, DE
16 June 2015